How I Feel

I Feel Afraid

By Connor Stratton

level 2

little blue readers

www.littlebluehousebooks.com

Little Blue House is distributed by North Star Editions:
sales@northstareditions.com | 888-417-0195

Produced for Little Blue House by Red Line Editorial.

Photographs ©: Shutterstock Images, cover, 4, 6–7, 11, 14–15, 17, 18, 23 (bottom), 24 (top right), 24 (bottom left); iStockphoto, 9 (top), 9 (bottom), 12, 21, 23 (top), 24 (top left), 24 (bottom right)

Library of Congress Control Number: 2020913840

ISBN
978-1-64619-293-9 (hardcover)
978-1-64619-311-0 (paperback)
978-1-64619-347-9 (ebook pdf)
978-1-64619-329-5 (hosted ebook)

Printed in the United States of America
Mankato, MN
012021

About the Author

Connor Stratton enjoys writing books for children and watching movies, such as *Inside Out*. He's always trying to understand his feelings better. He lives in Minnesota.

Table of Contents

Scary Sounds 5

Bad Dream 13

High Up 19

Glossary 24

Index 24

Scary Sounds

I hear a sound at night.

I don't know what made

the sound.

I feel afraid.

I cover my face with my blanket, but I still feel afraid.

blanket

I get out of bed and
look outside.

I hear the sound again.

The sound is coming from
the tree.

9

The tree is not scary.

I know I am safe, so I feel better.

Bad Dream

I have a bad dream.

It wakes me up, and I

feel afraid.

I find my mom.

She hugs me, and I know
I am safe.

15

I can go back to sleep because I feel better.

jungle gym

High Up

I'm at the playground.

I climb up high on the

jungle gym.

I look down, and the ground looks far away. I don't want to fall, and I feel afraid.

I call for my dad, and he helps me climb down.
I feel better when I know I am safe.

Glossary

blanket

playground

jungle gym

tree

Index

B
bed, 8

D
dream, 13

J
jungle gym, 19

S
sound, 5, 8